Other books by Norma Blackmon

A Bible Study in the Books of Galatians and Ephesians
Available at
www.tatepublishing.com/bookstore
Amazon.com
Barnesandnoble.com

From Thunder to the Throne Room and God's Amazing Grace.

Hebrews: A Bible Study

Norma Blackmon

WESTBOW
P R E S S®
A DIVISION OF THOMAS NELSON
& ZONDERVAN

WestBow Press books may be ordered through
booksellers or by contacting:

WestBow Press
A Division of Thomas Nelson & Zondervan
1663 Liberty Drive
Bloomington, IN 47403
www.westbowpress.com
1 (866) 928-1240

Because of the dynamic nature of the Internet, any web addresses or
links contained in this book may have changed since publication and
may no longer be valid. The views expressed in this work are solely those
of the author and do not necessarily reflect the views of the publisher,
and the publisher hereby disclaims any responsibility for them.

Any people depicted in stock imagery provided by Thinkstock are
models, and such images are being used for illustrative purposes only.
Certain stock imagery © Thinkstock.

ISBN: 978-1-4908-9690-8 (sc)
ISBN: 978-1-4908-9689-2 (e)

Print information available on the last page.

WestBow Press rev. date: 09/22/2015

Contents

Introduction ix

A Bible Study through Hebrews Questions 1

Priests are called by God 47

Coming to God His way 47

Complaining about our calling, position and/or status in service 48

A Bible Study through Hebrews Answers 49

Bibliography 73

*For my
Grandchildren;
Gwendolyn, Caleb, Nathan,
Rachel, and Lucas.*

*May you always live in the Spirit's truth, walk in the
Savior's light, and rest in the Father's love.
I am so glad that God allowed for
me to be your grandma!*

I was very pleased to review Norma Blackmon's Study in Hebrews Bible Study. I believe this book will be a powerful tool to aid in personal and group bible study. It is evident that the study can be done at any given pace and Norma's well thought out questions and answers will naturally lead to many lively discussions. As I worked my way through each chapter, I was personally challenged to look deeper into God's Word. Can't wait for the next book!

Pastor Stephen Gonzales
Senior Pastor
Presence of the Lord Christian Church
Corona, California

"As with Norma's previous work on Galatians and Ephesians, this study will force you to focus directly upon the text of scripture that is before you, a discipline that other studies lack. There are no rabbit trails here, which as a Pastor, is very refreshing to encounter! Additionally, any group can benefit from this study, as it is simple enough for the young and direct enough to keep any group growing in their understanding of the deep truths of God! I am glad to commend Norma for her diligence and to recommend this work to you, for the blessing of your group and the furtherance of His Kingdom!"

Pastor Frank Sanchez

This amazing study through Hebrews really gets one into God's Word. It forces you to read and understand the practical implications of following Christ. We need to be getting directly into His Word, and be ready for what is coming our way, to prepare our minds so that we can hear God speaking to us. Norma has written a study on Galatians & Ephesians too... I can't wait 'til she writes studies for every book of the Bible!

Jackie Neff, 89.7 KSGN

Introduction

Welcome to A Bible Study through the book of Hebrews, taken from the New King James version. This timeless book, for me, really brings together the Old and New Testaments as we read and learn about the priesthood, the high priest, **our** High Priest, the law, Melchizedek, the saving grace we have in our Lord and Savior Jesus Christ, and so much more. The boldness now afforded to us to approach the mercy seat of God for help, and our King who lives to make intercession for us daily.

We read of faith, of obedience, of things seen and unseen, and of God's perfect provision that, from the beginning of time, has made a way to sustain us and keep us as we live a life set apart for Him.

Why did Noah build the ark, and what had never been seen before? What did Abraham do with his spoils after he rescued Lot? What does it mean to have faith? Truly.

This bible study in the book of Hebrews is a wonderful inductive style study that puts you, the reader, immediately and directly into the bible. I encourage you to read through each chapter first before you answer the chapter's questions. So often we are quick to read ahead of ourselves and then struggle to understand what we have just read. This study provides for the reader to go through each chapter, often times verse by verse, as quickly or as thoughtfully as each would desire. Rich with dozens of accompanying scriptures to look up, we are provided a wonderful opportunity to dig in and search God's word, not only helping us to learn our bible, but aids in our understanding as we seek to apply God's truths and direction to our lives. If you are new to bible studies, I encourage you to look at the answers in the back of the book, as this will not only help you to fall into the rhythm of reading each verse, but offers fresh and practical application so that we, as God calls us, may be equipped for every good work. I am so excited for you!

May our beautiful Savior meet you right where you are as you pray, and read, and work through this bible study. And may we evermore be transformed more and more into the image of our Jesus. What more could we ever ask for?

Enjoy!

Hebrews Chapter 1

Questions

1) Who spoke at various times and in various ways? _____
2) How did He speak to the fathers?

_____

3) Look up the following verses and write down some of the various ways that God spoke.
   Numbers 12:4-8; Genesis 31:11; 46:2. You also have all the prophets. Read Isaiah 1:1; Ezekiel 1:1-3; Daniel 7:1; Exodus 3:1-17.

_____

Let me add that these are all incredible books to be read and cherished in their entirety (as is all scripture), not just to pick out a few verses. All of God's word is so pertinent to our lives today. Not only for the times we are living in for strength, courage, council, hope, direction and correction, but to keep us ever mindful of the Majesty, the Sovereignty, and the incredible grace of our God, and His faithfulness to meet and lead and provide for His people.

4) How has God spoken to us in these last days?

_____

5) Whom has God appointed heir of all things? _____
6) Through whom did God make the world? _____
7) Who *is* the brightness of God's glory and the express image of His person? _____
8) Our very lives should be a model of God's truths. Our every thought, word, deed, and motive should be a testimony to all that we are followers of the risen Christ. What do you notice in verse 3 about Jesus? As we are called to be examples of, or a reflection of, Jesus is the _____.
   Read John 1:1, 14; Colossians 1:15; 2 Corinthians 4:3, 4.
9) Who is upholding all things by the word of His power? Read John 1:3; Colossians 1:16, 17.

_____

10) Who has purged our sins and now sits at the right hand of the Majesty on high?

_____

11) Who has obtained a more excellent name than the angels?

_____

12) In verse 5, who is the begotten Son? _____

13) In verse 6, who is to Be worshipped? _____

14) Still in verse 6, who are called To worship? _____

15) In verse 7, who are called to minister? _____
   There are those who would put Jesus in the same category as the angels, and not as He is, the only begotten Son of God, and that is the distinction the author is making with these statements. There can be no confusing the two. One is God, the other created beings. Psalm 104 is a list of created things and you will notice that angels are included.

16) In verse 9, who has God anointed? _____

17) In verse 10, who laid the foundation of the earth? _____

18) Read verses 10, 11. What will perish and who will remain? Read also 2 Peter 3:10-13.

_____

19) In verse 12, whose years will not fail? _____

20) To whom did God say, "Sit at My right hand"? _____

21) Read verses 13, 14. Who are the ministering spirits? _____

_____

22) Who are they sent to minister to? _____

Hebrews Chapter 2

Questions

1) Therefore, understanding that Jesus is not a created being or an angel, He is God, we must give more *intensely serious* attention to what?

_____

2) Still in verse 1, what are we in danger of if we are not serious

_____

    In the original King James Version it reads, 'lest any time we should let them (the things we have heard) slip.' To slip here means to be forgotten or to let something (the opportunity for salvation?) slip away from us. Lest the salvation which we heard how to obtain escape us.

3) What is the *word* in verse 2 referring to?

_____

4) According to verse 2, who was the *word spoken through*? You can also read Acts 7:53; Galatians 3:19.

_____

5) Read verses 2, 3. What is Paul afraid we might neglect in verse 3?

_____

Read also Hebrews 10:28, 29.

    If disobeying the message of the law brought punishment, and that message was delivered by *(just)* angels, how greater a punishment should we receive if we reject the message of grace and forgiveness and the salvation that was spoken of, and offered by, Jesus Christ, the Son of God?

    Again, we see the author making an important distinction between Jesus and the angels.

6) Who first spoke of this salvation? You can also read Matthew 4:17; John 4:13, 14; 6:27, 29, 32-40. _____

7) Looking back to chapter 1, who is the Lord? Be thoughtful and write down some of what we read in chapter 1 that speak to who He is and what He has done.

_____

_____

8) Back to Hebrews chapter 2. Picking up in verse 3, who confirmed that Jesus spoke of this salvation?

_____

9) Who else bore witness? _____

10) In what ways did God bear witness?

_____

You can also read Acts 2:22, 43; 5:12; 14:3; 15:12.

11) In verse 5, we are reminded once again that Christ is superior to the angels. What are we told is *not* put in subjection to the angels?

_____

12) A) According to verse 8, what do we not yet see?

_____

B) What does *not yet* imply?

_____

13) According to verse 9 who do we see?

_____

14) What do verses 7 and 9 both say of Jesus?

_____

15) Why was Jesus made like man, a little lower than the angels? Read also Hebrews 2:14.

_____

16) Who is the captain of our salvation?

_____

17) Who is He who sanctifies?

_____

18) Who are those who are being sanctified?

_____

19) What does Jesus now call them (us)?

_____

20) In verse 13, who does Jesus put His trust in?

_____

21) Read again verses 9, 10, 14 and answer the following questions.
   A) According to verse 14, who had the power of death?

   _____

   B) What has Jesus done to him? _____

   Jesus paid the penalty for our sin, death (remember Romans 6:23, the wages of sin is death), and by doing so He has abolished death for all who believe and are under the blood of the Lamb. See 2 Timothy 1:8-10.
   C) What are we told in 1 Peter 5:8? _____

   _____

22) Why, according to verse 15, were these people in bondage?

   _____

23) What were they afraid of?

   _____

24) A) According to Revelation 1:18, who has the keys of Hades and Death? B) Who gave His life for you? _____
25) Who does the Son *not* give aid to?

   _____

26) Who *does* the Son give aid to?

   _____

27) Who (are) the seed of Abraham? You can also read Galatians 3:7, 29.

   _____

28) Read verses 17-19. How, or why, is Jesus able to aid those who are tempted?

   _____

   Jesus experienced all that a person goes through. He knows how difficult it can be to obey God completely. Read Mark 14:34-36; Luke 22:41-44. He understands temptation (remember He was tempted in the wilderness), Matthew 4:1-11. And still He lived a life in complete and absolute obedience to the Father, being perfect and living a sinless life.
29) Read Exodus 19:10-13, and then read Hebrews 4:16. What a contrast! What has Jesus now made possible for those who have received Him and put their trust in Him?

   _____

   _____

Hebrews Chapter 3

Questions

1) Chapter 3 begins again with *'therefore'* or *'and so'* or *'or because of'*, building on what has been written in the previous verses. Who is the author addressing in verse 1?

   _____

2) What is he calling us to do? _____

3) Who are we to consider? _____

4) Who was Jesus faithful to? You can also read John 4:34; 5:30; 6:38; Luke 22:42.

   _____

5) Still in verse 2, who else was also faithful *in His entire house*?

   _____

6) Who is the One in verse 3? _____

7) According to verse 4, who has built all things? _____

8) What are we told about Moses in verse 5a? You can refer back to Exodus 39:32-43; 40:16.

   _____

9) What house is Christ faithful over? _____

10) Verse 6 says *we* are this house if what?

    _____

11) 11) Verse 7 offers a conditional choice. What is it? _____

12) According to verse 8, what happened in the wilderness?

    _____

13) Read verses 7-11 and answer the following questions.
    Verse 7: What opportunity was given? _____
    Verse 8: What were they exhorted not to do? _____
    Verse 9: What did their fathers do? _____
    Verse 9: What did their fathers see? _____
    Verse 10: Where did they always go astray? _____
    Verse 10: What have they not known? _____
    Verse 11: What did God swear? _____

14) Read verse 9 again. How do you think it is possible to see God's works and not know His ways? You can read verse 8 again.

_____

15) What specifically are we warned against in verse 12?

_____

16) Still in verse 12, what would result from unbelief?

_____

Remember this letter is written predominately to new believers (the brethren) who are in danger of falling away from the fellowship of and salvation in Jesus Christ.

17) What is the author of Hebrews calling for us to do in verse 13 and why? _____

18) What might we become in verse 14, and again, on what condition?

_____

19) Who were those that Moses led out of Egypt?

_____

20) What happened to them and why?

_____

21) What *rest* is the author referring to in this passage, verse 18?

_____

You can also read Deuteronomy 12:9, 10; Joshua 21:43-45.

For some wonderful history, read the following verses. In Genesis 12:5-7; 13:14-17; 15:7, 18-21 God talks to Abraham. In Deuteronomy 1:6-8, 21, 26, 27, 29-33, we read of Israel's unbelief. In Numbers 13:17-20, 27-29 (you can also see back to Genesis 15:18-21), we read that God had named these peoples specifically, centuries before, and would drive them out from before the children of Israel. In Numbers 14:6-11, 22-24, 26-38, we read that because of their unbelief, they were not allowed to enter into the Promised Land, save for Caleb and Joshua, who did believe God for what He promised He would do. Notice why they wandered in the wilderness for 40 years in Numbers 14:34. *One year* for every day they spied out the land.

22) Why couldn't these Israelite's whom God delivered from bondage enter this rest according to verse 19? _____

23) Look back to verse 12. Why did they depart from God? _____

Do you struggle with unbelief? Maybe in your relationships, or in your finances? Maybe just really believing that God is able to save and willing to forgive? Let Him know you are having a hard time, He knows it anyway. Confess that you understand that you do not really trust Him, that you *do* want to enter His rest, His peace. It is hard at times to live by faith, trusting in what you can't always touch or see. All of us have had these struggles, but we always have a choice in what we believe. God loves you, He cares for you, and He always will.

Hebrews Chapter 4

Questions

Chapter 3 ended with the author reminding his readers that because of unbelief, those who came out of Egypt *could not* enter into God's rest. You can read again of this *rest* in Deuteronomy 3:19; 12:10; 25:19. You can also read again of Israel's refusal to enter the land which God had promised them and the consequences in refusing to obey, to *trust* God. Numbers 13:17-21, 26-29, 30-33; 14:26-30.

1) According to verse 1, what still remains? _____

2) According to verse 2, what was preached? _____

3) In verse 2, who was the gospel preached to? _____
    _____

4) Still in verse 2, did they hear it? _____. Hebrews 3:16.

5) Even though the children of Israel heard the good news of God's rest, why did it not profit them? _____
    _____

6) According to verse 3, who enters God's rest?
    _____

7) Read verses 4-9. The idea of rest was first spoken of in Genesis 2:2, so we have an understanding of a rest. Read each of the following verses and fill in the blanks. In verse 6 we read

    A) Those to whom it was first preached _____

    B) Enter because of _____

    C) In verse 7 we read that 'after a long time later' David, in Psalm 95 says _____,If you will hear His voice and not harden your hearts as was done in the wilderness, making the case that God's rest is still available for those who believe.

    D) Verse 9, what therefore still remains for the people of God? _____

8) What are we called to be in verse 11 and why?
    _____

9) What is the definition of diligent?

_____

10) Read the verses below that can make us mindful of areas that *all* believers can and do struggle with. What are some areas you might need to be more diligent in, and what are some tools that can help you? _____

_____

We *can* know that we are forgiven, that God chooses to remember our sins no more, as if they had never happened; Psalm 103:12; Jeremiah 31:34. Having a critical spirit; Matthew 7:1, 2. Faith; Luke 17:5. Understanding God's will; Ephesians 5:17. Unbelief; Hebrews 3:19. All believers struggle with different things at different times, and yet God loves us always and has given us every tool, every encouragement, and every bit of grace to help us, and, as we are told in Philippians 1:6, to complete the work that He has begun in each of us.

11) How is the word of God described in verse 12, and what is it a discerner of?

_____

12) According to verse 13 is there anything hidden from God?

_____

13) Read Romans 14:10-12; 2 Corinthians 5:10, and again Hebrew 4:13. What does the author tell us we must do?

_____

You can also read Romans 14:13, and then Romans 14:1-8. What a wonderful thing to remember.

In the past few verses we have looked at ourselves, hopefully honestly, and acknowledged areas that we need to make better efforts in, be it keeping the faith, obedience, showing grace (the opposite of fault finding and criticisms), and not giving in to the lies of the devil, but holding fast the confession of our faith to the end. We have also taken a peek at our thoughts and motives, verse 12, and are reminded that however we might look to those around us, especially in certain circles, our hearts are always exposed before God. Often times we deceive ourselves into thinking that we can hide certain behaviors or rationalize our opinions and/or actions towards one another. Not so. God sees and hears everything (Matthew 12:36), and it is Him to whom we will give an account of ourselves. Not our spouse, not our boss, not our friends, or even our church.

Now remember I told you we would all be convicted in this study, and that is a wonderful thing. It means that God is reaching down and lifting us up, meeting us where each of us is and doing a work, His faithful work, in all of our lives (remember Philippians 1:6). God does not want anything to come between Him and His children, and often times it is hard to face His correction. But just as any parent corrects the child they love, so does our heavenly Father (Proverbs 3:12).

Our study does not stop here though. As we all have probably experienced sometime in our walk, we can feel far from God, disappointed in ourselves and unsure how to continue. And once again, God meets us with the good news.

14) A) What do we have according to verse 14?

B) Who is He? _____

C) What has He done? _____

15) Still in verse 14, because we have a High Priest, what are we encouraged to do?

_____

16) According to verse 15 what does our High Priest do for us and why is He able?

_____

17) A) In Hebrews 7:25, who is Jesus able to save? B) What does He do for them?

_____

_____

18) Since we have this High Priest, our Lord and Savior Jesus Christ, Who intercedes on our behalf before the Father, what can we now do according to Hebrews 4:16?

_____

Hebrews Chapter 5

Questions

1) Read verse 1 and fill in the blanks. What are we told about the high priest?
   - A) He is _____
   - B) From _____
   - C) And _____
   - D) For _____
   - E) That he may offer both _____
   - F) For _____

2) In verse 2, why can the priest have compassion of those who are ignorant or going astray?

   _____

   I love looking up the meaning of words in the scriptures in the Strong's Concordance as they give such understanding that I might better be able to apply God's truths.

   Compassion is defined as; moderate in passions, especially anger or grief. One who is not unduly (excessively) disturbed by the errors, faults or sins of others, but bears them gently. I am reminded of such verses as Galatians 6:1; Ephesians 4:1, 2; 2 Timothy 2:24, 25. Our pastors and elders have such a special calling to love and to bear. Pray for them always.

   Ignorant means lack of knowledge, understanding or education, *unaware of something.* Ignorance is different from transgressions, which is *intentional* and is defined as overstepping a limit (established by God), violating a law, command, or moral code. Read Numbers 15:22-31.

3) In verse 3, because of his (man's) weaknesses, what is required of him?

   _____

   You may read of these requirements in Leviticus 16:6, 11, 15-17.

4) According to verse 4, does any man take the honor of priesthood to himself?

   _____

5) Who is he called by? _____
   For some wonderful reading on this you can read Exodus 28:1; Numbers 8:5-14. Aaron is from the tribe of Levi and was called by God to serve as priest, both him and his sons. The rest of the Levites were called to minister *to* the priest and *in* the Tabernacle. This was their calling, their inheritance, given to them by God, for His purpose and His service. Numbers 18:2-7, 21-24

6) Read verses 5 and 6. In verse 5 did Jesus call Himself to the priesthood? _____

7) Still in verses 5 and 6, A) Who called Him and B) What does He say of Him in verse 6?

   _____

8) Read through verse 7 and answer the following questions
   A) Who did Jesus offer prayers and supplications to? __
   B) Who was able to save Him from death? _____
   C) Why was He heard? _____

9) What does verse 8 tell us that Jesus learned and how?

   _____

   To learn is to acquire or possess knowledge through experience. Obedience is recognized or manifested through ones compliance or submission. So we understand that, through experience, Jesus learned (acquired or possessed knowledge of) obedience (submission) because of the things He suffered. And again, because of His sufferings, or, because of what Jesus went through, (partook of, experienced), He understands fully how difficult obedience (submission) can be. Read again Hebrews 2:18; 4:15.

10) Finish the first part of verse 9. And having been _____
    Jesus is God, John 1:1, and therefore has always been perfect and righteous and just, and to imply otherwise is not the meaning here. The word perfect here is to *accomplish,* to *fulfill,* and to *finish.* Read what Jesus said in John 19:30, "It is finished".

    You can also read *to be found.* Jesus endured trials and temptations without sinning (1 Peter 2:18-22). He *is* perfect. Having been tempted, Jesus understands our weaknesses.

And being sinless (2 Corinthians 5:21; Isaiah 53:6, 9), He can go before the Father and make intercession for us. Jesus *is* our High Priest.

11) Still in verse 9, having been perfected, what has Jesus become and for who?

_____

12) In verse 10, again, who has called Jesus to be High Priest?

_____

13) What does the writer of Hebrews tell these believers they have become in verse 11?

_____

14) In verse 12, what does the author tell these believers they should be by now?

_____

To teach is to impart knowledge or skill to somebody by instruction or example. I would submit to you that the greatest teaching moments in our lives are not when we are talking, but when we are doing. When you excuse yourself from those telling hurtful jokes or gossiping, when you change the channel or decline to go see a certain movie. When you reach out to a struggling brother or sister in Christ instead of condemning them; when you know that you do not have the answers yet you are there with one who is hurting. When you are ministering to the unlovable and remembering the forgotten, by our examples, by our lifestyle, we are all teachers.

15) Still in verse 12, read the verse a couple of times and fill in the following. I know the writers words are pretty harsh and can certainly sting, even cutting us to the heart (remember chapter 4:12). But that is okay! Isn't that why we do bible studies? So we can learn and grow and be changed? So hang in there! Don't ever give up!!

    A) What do these believers need?

_____

    B) What do they need to be taught again?

_____

    C) What have they come to need?

_____

16) Notice the word *come*. To *come* to something can be the result of something. As a result of being *dull of hearing* (verse 11), how does the author describe them in verse 13?

_____

Unskilled does not necessarily mean that they lacked instruction in righteousness, but lacked experience because they did not practice it.

17) In the context of these verses, what type of believer might *those who are of full age* be referring to in verse 14? _____

18) Still in verse 14, how have their *senses* been exercised to discern both good and evil?

_____

Hebrews Chapter 6

Questions

1) Verse 1 starts with therefore, or *because of,* or *and so,* and continues the context of the previous chapter and verses with regards to our spiritual growth, our faith, our obedience in righteousness, and our ability to rightly discern good and evil. What are we told in verse 1 that we should be leaving, and what should we be going on to?

_____

_____

Elementary: Encompassing or involving only the most simple of basic facts or principles, requiring little skill or knowledge. *Foundation:* The beginning step, the initial or first level of support for building an idea.

2) Verse 1 and 2 list 6 of these elementary principles. What are they? Do not lay again the foundation of

A) _____

B) _____

C) _____

D) _____

E) _____

F) _____

As we look at these principles, it is important that we keep everything in its proper context so as not to lose sight of the authors intended instructions. The meaning of principles in these verses is 'the beginning' or 'origin'. Similarly the word 'foundation' refers to 'beginnings' or 'first principles'. The discussion of faith and resurrection and eternal judgment each have a place in Christian and evangelical conversations. What the author of Hebrews is addressing, I believe, is that these believers have no more understanding of these truths than when they first became Christians. They have not grown, they have not exercised their faith, and they have become *dull of hearing.*

3) What a wonderful opportunity scripture gives us to, if necessary, once again address any of these principles that some of us, or all of us, might still have questions about or struggles with. God has kept nothing back from us as He calls us to understand His word and obedience. What are we told in 2 Timothy 3:16, 17? _____

_____

_____

Read again verses 1-3. Dead works here refers to the law, and coming to understand that these *works* could not make us righteous before God. Read Romans 8:2, 3; Galatians 2:16,21. *Faith.* We are saved by grace through faith in Christ Jesus; Ephesians 2:8, 9; Galatians 3:22-24; Romans 5:1,2; Hebrews 11:6. We are justified (declared righteous), through faith in Christ alone. There are no works that we can do that will ever equal what Jesus accomplished on our behalf on the cross. You can also read Romans chapters 3 and 4, as well as Galatians chapters 2 and 3 for more reading on faith and works. *Baptisms* can be speaking of the baptisms in the New Testament, Matthew 3:3-17; Acts 2:41; 9:17,18; 16:25-34, and/or the Old Testament ritual washings prescribed by the Mosaic law and practiced by the Jewish people to be washed or cleaned. Numbers chapter 19, Lev. 11:24, 25; 16:23-28; Mark 7:1-4.

Laying on of hands was practiced in the Old Testament to commission someone into service. Read Numbers 27:18-20,23; Acts 13:2,3; 6:3-6; 1 Timothy 4:14. Often time's hands were laid on believers for them to receive the Holy Spirit such as in Acts 8:17; 19:6. At another time while Peter was still speaking, the Holy Spirit fell on those who had heard the word and received it, Acts 10:44-48. We are in God's hands, not mans.

Resurrection of the dead was spoken of in the Old Testament in Isaiah 26:19, Daniel 12:2, as well as several times in the New Testament. 1 Corinthians 15:12-23; Acts 24:15. *Eternal Judgment* There are two judgments referred to in the scriptures. One speaks of the condemnation on unbelievers, or the Great White Throne Judgment in Revelation 20:11-15. And one in which Jesus will decide every believers reward, Revelation 22:12; 1 Corinthians 3:8, 11-15.

Let's look at some more verses that might speak to some of our thoughts and/or questions. Read again Hebrews 5:14 and 2 Corinthians 13:5. Are we walking in faith? Are we exercising our faith by trusting God in all of our circumstances, by believing that He is able to save, the He does choose to forgive us our sins when we ask, the He will never leave us, and that He is able to do as He promises? We have been given faith to believe, Ephesians 2:8; Romans 12:3, it is up to us to walk in it. Hebrews 7:25 able to save; 1 John 1:9 faithful to forgive; Jude 24 able to present us blameless; Psalms 103:12; Jeremiah 31:34 chooses to forget; Philippians 1:6 able to complete what He has begun; Romans 4:21 able to do what He has promised; Philippians 4:19 able to supply all our needs.

How are we able to stand fast in the faith and persevere? By the power of God! 2 Timothy 1:7, God has given us power and strength. 1 Corinthians 2:4, 5, faith is in the power of God not man. Romans 15:13, we abound in hope by the power of God. Acts 1:8, we have the power to be witnesses. John 6:39; 10:27-30; 17:12, we will not be lost. We are His and He will never let go.

4) Read Hebrews 6:4-6 a few times. How does the author describe these particular followers?
    A) As those who were _____
    B) And have _____
    C) And have become _____
    D) And have _____
    E) And the _____ of the age to come.

5) According to verse 6, what is impossible for those who were *once enlightened* if they fall away?

_____

6) Still in verse 6, when these *believers* reject Christ, what are they doing?

_____

7) Who do you think can cause more damage and hurt to the name of Jesus? Someone who has never believed and continues to reject Him? Or someone who claimed to have been a follower but now believe something else and have turned from the truth, and why? _____

_____

8) Read verses 7, 8. The author uses an analogy of sorts to bring home his meaning in the previous verses. Remember also this is a predominately Jewish audience who has a deep understanding of agriculture so it is often times used as a reference in scripture to clarify meaning.

    A) What happens to the land that bears useful herbs?

_____

You can also read Psalm 65:9, 10.

    B) What happens to the land that bears thorns?

_____

You can also read Isaiah 5:1-6.

    There is a lot to take in from verses 4-8, and there are differing opinions on its meaning as well. Some view this as a hypothetical argument used to warn the spiritually immature. Some use this to make the case that you can lose your salvation. Still others believe these verses deal with a believer losing his rewards, but not his salvation.

    With regards to losing your salvation, I think the scripture is pretty clear. In Matthew 7:22, 23 Jesus says, "I never knew you". Not," I knew you and you left." Also in John 6:37-40; 10:28-30 Jesus tells us that all that the Father has given Him He has kept, and no one can snatch us from Him, neither from the Father's hand. How much more secure could we get?!! Don't confuse this with those who profess to be saved but are really not. Scripture is full of warnings about false prophets and false teachers and wolves in sheep's clothing. But for those who have truly come to Christ, they are, we are, His. As far as losing our rewards, this is spoken of in 1 Corinthians 3:5-15. Read again Hebrews 6:8 and see how the authors writes, *it* is rejected and *near* to being cursed. Not cursed. Rejected here is disqualified (read 1 Corinthians 9:27), and the Greek meaning is <u>disapproved after testing.</u> Remember too that these verses speak of what the land has produced, not the land itself. And again, when we read in 1 Corinthians 3:12, 13, we read of the believer's works and how they will be revealed by fire, of what sort it is. We read that some are of straw and wood, while others are of precious stones. Some will endure testing, while still others will burn. But the believer himself will be saved. These building materials we read of refer to the quality of the work and perhaps one's motivation as well. We could do an entire study on these verses, and I am sure I am not qualified. I can only share what I believe they mean and will leave it there.

9) Following the strong words of verse 8, in verse 9 the author tells these believers that even though he spoke in such a manner, he is what?

_____

10) In verse 10, what does the author tell them God is not unjust to forget?

_____

11) Still in verse 10, what work is he specifically referring to?

_____

12) What is the author's desire in verse 11?

_____

13) Who are we to imitate according to verse 12?

_____

14) Read verses 13 -15, *Abraham did patiently endure.* Now read Genesis 12:4; 21:5. From the time of God's promise until Isaac was born, how long did Abraham wait? _____

15) Read again verses 13-18. God made a promise and confirmed it by an oath, by two immutable things. Because of this, what do we have according to verse 18?

_____

16) How is this hope described in verse 19?

_____

17) Who is our High Priest according to verse 20?
18) Who is the Presence behind the veil?

_____

Remember the veil is what separated the Holy Place from the Most Holy Place. The Most Holy Place or the Holy of Holy's was the place where God dwelt. Where the priest only entered once a year, Exodus 30:10, and where the Ark of the Covenant and the mercy seat were placed, Exodus 26:31-34; Leviticus 16:2.

Hebrews Chapter 7

Questions

1) Read Hebrews 7; 1-3 several times and write down as many things as you can about Melchizedek. _____

_____

   We are going to take the above verses and break them down with scriptures of the Old Testament as we continue to grow in our understanding of scripture and history, always appreciating how God has always gone before His chosen and made a way for them, and for us. Too often our expectations are set and when God does visit us and/or bring revelation, we miss it, or worse, ignore it. In these verses, in this whole book actually, we too can gain so much as we understand not only the absoluteness of salvation through Jesus Christ, but His validity as High Priest.

2) Read again verses 1, 2, and then read Genesis 14:5-7, 11-16, 18-20. According to Genesis 14:14, why did Abram (later called Abraham), go to war?

_____

3) In Genesis 14:16, what did Abram bring back?

_____

4) In Genesis 14:20, what did Abram do with part of his *spoils?*

_____

5) Back to Hebrews 7:2, what did Abraham give to Melchizedek?

_____

6) Still in verse 2 what are the translations of Melchizedek?

_____

Melchizedek *means* King of righteousness, just like Moses *means* drawn. It is a name. Jesus *is* our righteousness.

   Salem *means* peace and is thought to be the ancient name of Jerusalem.

   This peace is a place, not a state of being. Melchizedek is the king of a place whose name means peace. Jesus Christ *is* our peace. Read John 16: 33; Philippians 4:6.7.

The children of Israel, brought up under the Aaronic priesthood, struggled with the notion that Jesus could be a priest since He was from the tribe of Judah and not of the Levites, as the Law of Moses and the first covenant commanded.

7) What are we told about Melchizedek in the first part of verse 3?

_____

These verses do not mean that Melchizedek had no father or mother, just that there was no genealogy written for him in the book of Genesis. Notice also in verse 3 it reads, *like the Son of God.* You cannot be *like* someone and *be* that someone at the same time.

8) What does scripture tell us about being in the priesthood in Nehemiah 7:61-64?

_____

9) Back to Hebrews chapter 7, what does the last part of verse 3 tell us?

_____

10) What do the scriptures tell us about being in the priesthood in Numbers 8:23-26?

_____

11) Keep in mind that the previous scriptures all deal with the Aaronic priesthood and the requirements established for that priesthood. Look back to Hebrews 6:20. What are we told about Jesus becoming our High Priest? According to what?

_____

_____

12) According to Hebrews 7:5, who receives the priesthood? ___

_____

13) What is the commandment for them under the law? _____

_____

14) Who are they to receive tithes from? _____
You can also read Numbers 18:21-24.

15) According to Hebrews 7:6, who received tithes from Abraham though he was not of the tribe of Levi? _____

16) In verse 11, what did the people receive under the Leviticus priesthood? _____

17) Still in verse 11, since perfection did not come through the Leviticus priesthood, what was needed? _____

_____

You can also read Galatians 2:16; 3:21-25; Romans 7:6.
18) In verse 12 we read 'for the priesthood being changed', *read removed, Hebrews 12:27,* what other change was necessary?

_____

Remember the Levites taught the law. If the priesthood is removed, so is the law in its form. This law is based on man's ability to meet its requirements, which we cannot do. We needed a better way, a permanent way, and that way was made for us in Jesus. For God's clear understanding on this, read (and commit to heart) Romans 8:3, 4.
19) Who is the 'He' spoken of in verse 13? _____
20) Which tribe is our Lord from according to verse 14? _____
21) Had Moses spoken anything about the priesthood and the tribe of Judah? _____
22) Which tribe had been given the duties of the priesthood?

_____

23) Read verses 18, 19. What was the former commandment?

_____

24) According to verse 18, why was it annulled, or *made invalid?*

_____

25) How does verse 16 refer to the law?

_____

See also Romans 8:3.
26) What does verse 19a tell us of the former commandment?

_____

27) Read Romans 8:3, 4. According to verse 4, what did Jesus do that we could not do?

_____

28) Still in Romans 8:4, who is this fulfilled in? _____
29) What are we told in Romans 8:1?

_____

_____

30) Back to Hebrews 7:20. Was Jesus made priest with or without an oath?

_____

31) In verse 21, what was the oath that God has sworn?

_____

32) Read verse 22, and 16. Why has Jesus become a *better covenant?*

_____

_____

You can also read Romans 8:11; Ephesians 1:19, 20.
33) In verse 23, why were there many priests?

_____

34) Why did Jesus have an unchangeable priesthood?

_____

35) What did Jesus not need to do according to verse 27?

_____

36) Still in verse 27, what did the priests offer sacrifices for?

_____

You can also read Leviticus 9:7; 16:6-11, 15.
37) What did Jesus do once and for all, and in the context of the previous verses, what exactly does that mean?

_____

38) In verse 28, who did the *law* appoint as high priests and how are they described?

_____

39) Still in verse 28, Who, by the word of the oath, has been appointed forever and how is He described? _____

_____

Hebrews Chapter 8

Questions

1) According to verse 1a, what is the author's main point with regards to what he had previously written? _____
_____

You can see back to chapter 7:23-28.

2) Verse 1 says we have *just such* a High Priest. Who is our High Priest? _____

3) According to Hebrews 7:20, 21, how does He differ from those that were before Him?
   A) Jesus was made priest _____
   B) They have become priests _____

4) Read Hebrews 7:23-28 and fill in the blanks.
   A) There were many priests because they were prevented
   _____

   B) But Jesus, because He continues forever
   _____

   C) Therefore He is also able to
   _____

   D) Our High Priest is
   _____

   E) And has become
   _____

   F) Who does not need daily
   _____

   G) For the law appoints as high priests
   _____

   H) But the word of the oath appoints the Son who has been
   _____

   Such *is* our High Priest.

5) Back to Hebrews 8:3, why was it necessary that Jesus, our High priest, have something to offer?
   _____

Look up the following verses in Leviticus. Though just a sprinkling of Old Testament scripture (I always encourage all of us to read it in its entirety), you can read some of what was offered in these sacrifices, as well as taking note of why these sacrifices and offerings were necessary. And though temporary fixes at best since the blood of goats and bulls could never pay the debt we owed because of sin, God has always provided a way to restore fellowship with Him, and to keep us in His way until the promise of a better covenant was fulfilled. Remember, these are all from Leviticus. The burnt offering, 1:2, 3; 6:8-13. The grain offering, 2:1-3; 6:14-23. The peace offering, 3:1; 7:11-21. The sin offering, 4:1-3; 6:24-30. The trespass offering, 5:5-7; 7:1-7. The daily offering, Exodus 29:38, 39,42.

6) Read Eph. 5:2. What did Jesus our High Priest offer?

_____

7) Let's see how well you memory is. Read verse 4 a couple of times and answer the following questions.

    A) According to the law, which tribe served as priest?

    _____

    B) Of which tribe was Jesus? _____

8) According to the first part of verse 5, what did these priests serve?

_____

To serve here means to minister, the observance of rites and duties, especially religious, to perform sacred services.

9) Still in verse 5, what was Moses divinely instructed to make, and according to what?

_____

You can read Exodus 25:1, 2, 8, and 9.

10) According to verse 7, why was there a need for a second covenant?

_____

11) Read over verses 8, 9 and Exodus 19:5. According to verse 9, why did God find fault with the children of Israel with regards to the first covenant? _____

_____

12) In verse 10, God says He will put His laws in our minds and
_____ Read also Deuteronomy 30:6.

13) Read Exodus 31:18; 32:15, 16. On what did God write the Mosaic Law?

_____

14) What did God tell the children of Israel in Ezekiel 36:26, 27?

_____

_____

15) What, according to Hebrews 8:13, has the new covenant done?

_____

Hebrews Chapter 9

Questions

1) Read verses 1-3 and answer questions 1 and 2. What was in the first part of the tabernacle, and what was this area called

_____

_____

2) The second part of the tabernacle, the room behind the veil, was called what?

_____

This place is also called the Most Holy Place.

3) From verse 4, what was placed in the Most Holy Place, and what was kept in it?

_____

4) Daily, as the Lord instructed, the priests would minister in the Holy Place. According to verse 7, how often and in what manner did the high priest enter the Most Holy Place?

_____

5) Still in verse 7, for what purpose did the high priest enter the second part of the tabernacle, or the Holy of Holies? _____

_____

You can also read Leviticus 16:6-17, 29, 30, 34.

6) According to Hebrews 9:9, what were these sacrifices offered by the high priest unable to do?

_____

7) In verse 10, what were they concerned with?

_____

For more insight you can also read Mark 7:3-9, Matthew 15:8,9.

8) In verse 11, who came as High Priest? _____

9) Look back to verses 6 and 7, and take note of what the high priest offered, and where this took place. Now read over verse 12 and answer the following questions.

    A) Who has entered the Holy of Holies?

    _____

    B) What has He offered?

    _____

    C) What has He obtained once and for all?

    _____

    D) What does *once and for all* imply?

    _____

10) Read verse 14 along with verse 10, and Hebrews 6:1. What dead works is the author referring to? _____

As much as we *might* and *can* enjoy traditions and ceremonies, we must never neglect to remember that *works and rituals* could not, *cannot* bring life. The law revealed sin, Romans 3:20, and showed the people that they could not meet the righteous requirements of the law. In Christ those righteous requirements were met, Romans 8:2-4, and then He offered us *His* righteousness through faith in Him. See 2 Corinthians 5:21; Romans 10:4.

11) Read verse 15 and answer the following.

    A) What is Jesus a mediator of?

    _____

    B) By what means?

    _____

    C) What did He redeem us from?

        _____ (the curse of the law, remember James 2:10)

    D) That those who are called may receive what?

    _____

    Redemption, to be redeemed, is *to cause to be released by payment of a ransom, to be liberated, delivered by receipt of payment.* Jesus Christ *is* our Redeemer!

12) According to verse 17, when is a testament (will) in force?

_____

13) What was the first covenant dedicated with?

_____

14) Moses did several things that we read of in verse 19.

    A) What was the first thing Moses did?

    _____

    B) What did Moses do next?

C) Read Exodus 24:3, 7, 8. What took place (what did the people do), before Moses sprinkled the blood of the covenant on the people?

15) Read Hebrews 9:18-20, and then write out Matthew 26:28.

16) What else, according to verse 21, was sprinkled with the blood?

17) Verse 22a tells us that according to the law, almost all things are purified with blood. What else are we told in verse 22?

18) As I am writing this, I can't help but sing that great old hymn, "There is power, power, wonder working power, in the blood of the Lamb; there is power, power, wonder working power in the precious blood of the Lamb." Anyway, in verse 23 we read, but heavenly things themselves, *not the copies*, were purified with a better sacrifice. What sacrifice is the author referring to?

19) Verse 24 tells us that Jesus has appeared in the presence of the Father for us. In Hebrews 7:25 we read, 'He always lives to _____'.

20) What are we told about Jesus in Romans 8:34?

21) Back to Hebrews chapter 9, read verses 25, 26. What did Jesus *not* do that the high priest did, and why? _____

22) Read again verse 26 and fill in the blanks.
    A) But now

    B) He has appeared

    C) By the sacrifice of

23) According to verse 27, what is appointed to men, and what comes after? You can also read Matthew 13:24-30; 25:31-33; 2 Peter 2:4-9.

_____

24) As we learn from the scriptures that man dies only once (*Hebrews 9:27*), that Christ came in the likeness of men (*Philippians 2:7*), to do what we could not do *(Romans 8:3,4)*, and paid our debt *(Romans 6:23* 'the wages of sin is death'), we come to understand as we read again in verse 28 that Christ was offered _____

25) For those who eagerly wait, Christ will appear a second time for _____

Hebrews Chapter 10

Questions

1) What could the law *not* do?

_____

Read again Hebrews 9:9.
2) According to verse 3, what did the sacrifices offered under the law do?

_____

3) What could the blood of bulls and goats not do?

_____

4) Read verses 5-7. What does Jesus say He has come to do?

_____

5) A definition of will is; desire, pleasure, what one wishes or has determined shall be done. Read John 6:38-40; what is the will of the Father?

_____

You can also read John 3:16 and 2 Peter 3:9 that speak to us of God's great love for us.
6) In verse 9, what did God take away and why?

_____

You can also read Hebrews 8:8-13.
7) Why was it necessary for God to establish a second covenant according to Hebrews 8:7?

_____

Read again Hebrews 7:18, 19; Galatians 2:16; 3:11.
8) Read again verses 5-10. What *will* is verse 10 referring to?

_____

9) By that *will*, what has happened to us and how was that accomplished?

_____

10) Answer the following questions from verse 11.
   A) What is the position of the priest?

   _____

B) What does he repeatedly do?

_____

C) What can these sacrifices never do?

_____

Read again what we are told in Hebrews 9:9.
11) Answer the following questions from verse 12.
    A) Who is the Man?

_____

    B) What did He offer?

_____

    C) What did Jesus do after His offering?

_____

    D) Notice how the priest is standing and offering sacrifices daily. What might the significance of Jesus sitting down be?

_____

You can also read John 19:30.
12) Who has Jesus perfected forever?

_____

13) Read verses 17, 18, as well as verse 14, and chapter 9:12. Why is there no longer an offering for sin?

_____

You can read again John 1:29; 19:30 if you need to.
14) What is the veil spoken of in verse 20?

_____

Read Exodus 26:31-35; Matthew 27:50, 51.
15) Verse 1 tells us that *believers* now have the boldness to enter the Holiest. In Hebrews 9:23 we read about the *copies* of the heavenly things, that is *the Tabernacle,* constructed under God's direction by Moses and the children of Israel. Read Exodus 25:1-9, 22; 26:33, 34; 40:34-38. What was the Holiest, or the Most Holy Place in the tabernacle?

_____

16) Read again verses 19-22.
    A) According to verse 22b, before we could draw near, what was needed?

_____

See again Hebrews 9:21, 22.

B) How did the *copy* of these things accomplish this? __

_____

Read Exodus 30:20; Leviticus 16; 3, 4; Hebrews 9:13.
C) According to verse 19, how do we enter now? _____

_____

You can also read Hebrews 7:19; 9:14; Romans 5:1, 2.

17) In verses 22-25 we are given three exhortations and the manner in which to do them. Read the verses and fill in the following.

A) In verse 22 we are told to draw near

_____

B) In verse 23 we are told to hold fast

_____

C) In verse 24 we are told to

_____

D) In verse 22 how are we to draw near?

_____

E) In verse 23 how are we told to hold fast our confession?

_____

F) In verse 24 why are we to consider one another?

_____

18) What do you think it means to *consider* one another to *stir up good works?*

_____

19) Verse 25 gives us one of the best ways to consider and stir up one another. What is it?

_____

20) Continuing in verse 25, as we assemble together, and this doesn't just mean church, what else are we called to be doing and what do you think this means?

_____

21) Still in verse 25, what urgency does the author give this *exhortation?*

_____

22) What is the *Day* the author is referring to?

_____

23) According to verse 26, when does there no longer remain a sacrifice for sins?

_____

24) If we reject God's provision for salvation, what remains according to verse 27?

_____

25) Read James 4:4. According to Hebrews 10:27, who are the adversaries?

_____

Remember, we all have a choice. Read Joshua 24:15.

26) According to verse 28, what happens to anyone who rejects Moses' law, and by what testimony? _____

_____

27) Read verse 29 a few times and fill in the sentence. When we reject the incredible sacrifice of His Son, our Savior, according to verse 29 we...

    A) We _____
    To spurn, to treat with rudeness and neglect, with insult.

    B) We have _____
    To treat the blood of Christ no better than the blood of common man or animal sacrifices.

    C) We have _____
    Refers to the Holy Spirit. Read Matthew 12:31, 32.

28) Verse 30 is quoted from Deuteronomy 32:35, 36.

    A) What has God said?

    _____

    B) What did Jesus say in Luke 12:4, 5?

    _____

29) In Hebrews 10:32a, what is the author encouraging his readers to do?

_____

30) What does the author want them to remember?

_____

    I love the language in the King James translation. Personally I think it gives us a better picture to more fully appreciate many of the events written about in the scriptures. I also find it helps me to look up the definition of key words to, again, appreciate all that scripture has for us as we seek to grow, to endure, and be changed by the Word.

In verse 33 it reads; you *endured a great fight of afflictions.* **Endured:** to take patiently, to suffer, to remain, to not recede or flee, too bear bravely and calmly. **Great:** many, much, large. **Fight:** Combat, hard trial. **Afflictions:** Suffering or has suffered misfortune, calamity or evil.

31) What does verse 33a tell us about some of these sufferings?

_____

_____

In the King James it reads *made a gazing stock,* to bring upon the stage, set forth as a spectacle, theater, expose to contempt. Reproach means to revile, made to feel ashamed, disgraced.

32) Read the second part of verse 33 along with the first part of verse 34. Verse 33 tells us that along with their suffering, they *became companions.* The definition of companion is, partner, sharer, comrade. How was this applied in verse 34?

_____

_____

33) Still in verse 34, what did these believers know?

_____

You can also read Matthew 5:12; 1 Peter 4:13, 14.

34) What are these believers told to *not* do in verse 35?

_____

35) Read Hebrews 3:6; Philippians 1:6; Jude 24; 2 Corinthians 4:14; 1 Corinthians 6:14; John 6:40. What are we confident in?

_____

Hebrews Chapter 11

Questions

1) Verse 1 gives us a description of faith. Write out that description.

   _____

   Substance is what something is made up of. It is the nature or quality of; the foundation, assurance, confidence. The evidence of our faith is lived out in our lives every day; we endure, we hope, we wait.

2) According to verse 2, by what did the elders receive a good testimony?

   _____

3) Who are the elders the author refers to in verse 2?

   _____

4) What did they obtain and what do you think that means?

   _____

   _____

5) How does verse 3 tell us the world was *not* made?

   _____

6) Read Genesis 1:3, 6, 7, 9, 11, 14, 16, 17, 20, 24,........you get the idea. How *was* the world made?

   _____

7) According to verse 4, why was Abel's offering a more excellent sacrifice than Cain's?

   _____

   You can read of their offering in Genesis 4:1-7

8) By faith what did Enoch not see, and what testimony did he have in verse 5? _____

   _____

9) Write out the first part of verse 6.

   _____

10) What must those who come to God believe?

   _____

11) What was Noah <u>divinely warned of</u> in verse 7?

_____

12) Do you know what had not been seen before? _____
You can read Genesis chapters 6-11 to learn more about God's judgment, Noah, the Flood, the Rainbow, Noah's descendants, and more.

13) Still in verse 7, what *moved* Noah to build the ark?

_____

14) Because of his *obedience,* what did Noah become?

_____

15) In your own words, summarize what Abraham did by faith according to verse 8?

_____

_____

You can also read Genesis 12:1-3.

16) Read verses 9, 10. How does 9a describe the manner in which Abraham dwelt in the land of promise?

_____

17) In the second part of verse 9 we read Abraham, with Isaac and Jacob, dwelt in tents. What, if anything, does that imply to you?

_____

18) What is Abraham waiting for in verse 10?

_____

19) What city is verse 10 referring to?

_____

See Revelation 21:10.

20) What did Sarah receive through faith?

_____

21) Read verse 11 again. Why did Sarah have faith?

_____

22) Who is the *one man* in verse 12? _____

23) What do you think the meaning is behind *and him as good as dead?*

_____

24) What are we told about these believers in verse 13?
    A) They all died _____
    B) Not having _____
    C) But having seen them afar off _____
    D) And confessed that they were _____

25) Based on their confession in verse 13, according to verse 14, what have they declared?

    _____

26) What homeland are they seeking?

    _____

You can look back to verse 10.
27) How was Abraham tested?

    _____

28) Why do you think God tests His people?_____

    _____

Read Deuteronomy 8:2; 13:1-3
29) What did Abraham conclude according to verse 19? _____

    _____

30) Read verses 21-22 and Genesis 50:24-26. What did Joseph remind his brethren God would do in verse 24? _____

    _____

31) Read Genesis 50:25; Exodus 13:19. Who took the bones of Joseph with him out of Egypt?

    _____

In Genesis 49:29-50:14 you can read of the death and burial of Jacob, Joseph's father. You might notice how he was buried in Canaan, the Promised Land, as well as was Abraham and Sarah, Isaac and Rebekah, and Jacob's wife Leah.
32) Read Exodus 1:15-22 (esp. verse 17), along with Hebrews 11:23. What was the king's command?

    _____

You can read Exodus 1:1-14, for *why* the king made this command.
33) Read verses 24-27 a few times. How was Moses able to refuse Pharaoh, suffer affliction, and endure? _____
34) What does verse 25 refer to sin as? _____

35) According to verses 27-29, Moses was able to endure leaving Egypt without fear, keep the Passover, and cross through the Red Sea as on dry land because of what? _____

36) In verse 31, who perished? _____

37) Read verses 39, 40. According to verse 39, what did these believers obtain and through what?

_____

38) Still in verses 39 and 40, what did they *not* receive and why?

_____

For some wonderful scriptures you can read Hebrews 5:9; 2:10; 7:28. For another beautiful picture you can read Colossians 1:2-18.

Hebrews Chapter 12

Questions

1) Who is the *cloud of witnesses* referring to in verse 1?

_____

Read Romans 15:4; 1 Corinthians 10:11.
2) Verse 1 also tells us to lay aside *every weight,* and the *sin.* What do you think might be the difference between the two and why can it so easily ensnare us?

_____

Read 1 Corinthians 10:23.
3) What is the exhortation in the second part of verse 1?

_____

4) Verse 1 tells us to run the race with endurance. How does verse 2 tell us to do that?

_____

5) Still in verse 2, who *is* the author and finisher of our faith?

_____

6) Read verse 2 again along with verse 3 and complete the following from verse 3.
    A) Who are we to consider?

    _____

    B) What are we to consider?

    _____

    C) Why are we to consider?

    _____

To consider here is to look at our present sufferings in the light of what Jesus suffered on our behalf.
7) According to verse 8, what are we without chastening?

_____

8) According to verse 10, why does God chasten us?

_____

9) What does chastening yield according to verse 11?

_____

10) According to verse 14, what are we to pursue, and why is it important?

_____

  Pursue means to *seek after diligently* and to *earnestly endeavor to acquire.*

11) Read verses 15 and 16 and fill in the following
  A) We are to be looking carefully lest anyone

  _____

  B) Lest any root of

  _____

  C) Lest there be

  _____

12) Read verses 18-21 along with Exodus 19:10-19; 20:18-21. According to Exodus 19:11, what was God going to do? ____

_____

13) In Exodus 19:12, what would happen to anyone who touches the mountain?

_____

  Now read back in Hebrews 12:22-24 along with Hebrews 4:16.
  A) How do we come to the Father now? _____
  B) Is there any fear of death? _____

14) Read again Exodus 20:18. What does this verse tell us about the people as they witnessed the thundering and lighting?

_____

_____

15) In Exodus 20:20, what did Moses tell the people?

_____

16) Still in Exodus 20:20, what did Moses say that God has come to do and why?

_____

_____

17) Back to Hebrews chapter 12. Read verse 25 a few times thoughtfully. Read it again concentrating on the first half of the verse along with Hebrews 2:2, 3 and Numbers 14:20-24. In Numbers 14:23, what had happened and why?

_____

_____

18) Read the second half of Hebrews 12:25, along with Hebrews 10:26, 27. What is there for those who reject Jesus Christ?

_____

19) Back to chapter 12, read verses 26, 27. What does God say will be shaken?

_____

20) Read again Hebrews 12:27 along with Matthew 24:35. What will remain?

_____

21) Read Isaiah 65:17; Revelation 21:1, 2. What do we have to look forward to?

_____

22) As we are reminded in Hebrews 12:28 that we are receiving _a kingdom which cannot be shaken ,_ what are we to have and for what purpose? _____

_____

23) What we are told in 1 Peter 1:15? _____

_____

Hebrews Chapter 13

Questions

1) Read verses 1-3. What three exhortations are we given at the beginning of each of these verses?

    A) Verse 1

    _____

    B) Verse 2

    _____

    C) Verse 3

    _____

2) According to verse 5, what are we to be content with?

_____

3) Still in verse 5, what has our Father in heaven told us?

_____

4) What may we boldly say according to verse 6?

_____

You can also read Matthew 10:28; Luke 12:4,5.
5) Why can we say this?

_____

Read Romans 5:8-11; 8:33-39; Colossians 2:11-14.
6) Who is verse 7 referring to? _____

7) Read Numbers 23:19; James 1:17. What are we told about Jesus in Hebrews 13:8?

_____

8) Read verse 9 in the light of verse 8. Why is it so important that our hearts are established by grace? _____

_____

For more insight read Colossians 2:6-8; 20-23; Romans 14:17. Read Hebrews 13:10, 11 along with Leviticus 4:1-12; 13-21. Remember that the priests did not receive an inheritance with regards to land. Their portion was from God, Numbers 18:8-20.
Read verse 12 along with Matthew 27:31; Mark 15:20; Isaiah 53:7.

Read verses 13,14 along with Hebrews 11:24-26. Oh, may we have the heart of Moses.

9) According to verse 15, how often are we to offer praise to God? _____

10) In verse 16, with what sacrifices is God well pleased?

_____

11) What is the author's prayer request in verse 18a?

_____

12) Read verses 20,21. What is the author's prayer for his readers in verse 21. That we would be made what and for what purpose? _____

_____

13) What is the authors appeal to his readers in verse 22?

_____

14) How does the author close his letter in verse 25?

_____

Additional Scriptures for Hebrew Study

Enjoy

*******Priests are called by God.

Exodus 28:1 Aaron and his sons are called.
Numbers 3:10; Aaron and his sons are called
Numbers 3:5-9; The Levite's, the tribe of Levi, is called to the work of the tabernacle.
Numbers 3:14-17; Census of the Levite's.
Numbers 3:29, 31; Note specifically the family of Kohath and remember them.
Numbers 3:32; The Levite's serve under the priests.
Numbers 3: 40-45, 8:5-22; The tribe of Levi, the Levite's, are dedicated to God.
Note. Aaron is of the tribe of Levi yet God has called Aaron and his sons (and their sons after them), to serve as priests. His brethren, the Levites, will serve in the tabernacle.
Numbers 18:1-7; Duties of priests and Levites.
Numbers 18:20; Priests- no inheritance.
Numbers 18:21-24; Levites – tithes from the people.

******* Coming to God His way.

Lev. 10:1, 2; Aaron's sons die. They offered profane fire before God. In the King James Bible the language is 'strange' and can be defined as foreign, an enemy, or prostitute. Whatever it was, it was not in line with what God had commanded. I am reminded of Cain in Gen. 4:3-7. Cain and his brother Able had each brought offerings to the Lord. You would have to conclude that there had already been in place instruction with regards to offerings as it is mentions at other times long before the law was given. God did not accept Cain's offering, and speaks to him directly reminding him that *he knows what is right and to just do it* and all would be well. Isn't it something that to this day we are still trying to get to God on our own terms? We are reminded as well in the New

Testament that we should examine ourselves, both when we are bringing an offering and worship, Matthew 5:23,24, and when we are taking communion, 1 Corinthians 11:27-29.

*******Complaining about our calling, position and/or status in service.

Numbers 12:1-10; Aaron and Miriam had a problem with Moses's wife which in all probability was just an excuse to level a charge at and attack Moses. Miriam was a prophetess and would have had much standing, and of course Aaron, as priest, enjoyed quite a privileged position in ministering to the Lord. Yet they were jealous of the special relationship Moses had with God. I believe we should tread very carefully when we start to let our opinions of others move us to question whether someone can or should be in a specific position. We are called to be discerning, but I think we had better check our attitudes at the door about certain individuals and prayerfully consider how we might approach a situation like this. And only after we, with a pure heart, asked ourselves why we are questioning their position in the first place. Never should it be because we do not think this person or that person has any right or place to be in such positions because we do not like them or, be honest, because we do not think they are as fit as say, you or me. All things should solely rest in the authority of scripture.

Numbers 16:1-5; Remember Kohath from Num. 3; 29, 20. Continue through 8-11; 28-32, 35. As you read verse 35, remember back to verse 2 about the 250.

Read Luke 10:38–40; John 21:20–22. God has given each of us a heart, a calling, a place. We would do so much better if we spent our energy in a generous, loving obedience instead of comparing and complaining. How amazing that God would use us at all! Praise Him!

Hebrews Chapter 1

Answers

1) God the Father.
2) Through the prophets
3) Visions, dreams, signs, and face to face as it was with Moses.
4) His Son, Jesus.
5) Jesus.
6) Jesus.
7) Jesus.
8) Express image of His (God the Father) person.
9) Jesus.
10) Jesus.
11) Jesus.
12) Jesus.
13) Jesus.
14) The angels.
15) The angels.
16) Jesus.
17) Jesus.
18) The heavens and the earth. Jesus Christ.
19) Jesus.
20) Jesus.
21) Angels.
22) Those who will inherit salvation, believers.

Hebrews Chapter 2

Answers

1) What we have heard.
2) Drifting away.
3) The law.
4) Angels.
5) Salvation.
6) Jesus.
7) Our Lord and Savior Jesus Christ,. The Heir of all things through whom all that was made was made. The One who purged our sins and all the angels of God worship Him. His years will not fail. He **is** the only begotten Son of the Father.
8) Those who heard Him.
9) God.
10) With signs and wonders, with various miracles and gifts of the Holy Spirit.
11) The world to come.
12) A) All things under Jesus. B) It has not happened yet, but rest assured, it will happen.
13) Jesus.
14) He was made a little lower than the angels, in the likeness of man.
15) For the suffering of death that He, by the grace of God, might taste death for everyone. Read also verse 14a.
16) Jesus Christ.
17) Jesus Christ.
18) Believers.
19) Brethren
20) God the Father.
21) A) Satan. B) Jesus destroyed him. C) Be vigilant because your adversary the devil walks about like a roaring lion seeking whom he may devour. Vigilant means to be watchful and alert, especially to danger or to something that is wrong.
22) Because of fear.

23) Death.
24) A) Jesus Christ. B) Jesus Christ.
25) Angels.
26) The seed of Abraham.
27) Those that are of the faith.
28) In all things Jesus had to be made like His brethren. He Himself has suffered and been tempted. Yet he was perfect and therefore able to satisfy (make propitiation for), the requirements of a Holy God. So, in that He also has suffered, we can surely come to understand and appreciate as we read in Heb. 4:15 that we have a High Priest who Can sympathize with our weaknesses. This does not mean that our behaviors are condoned and we are without excuse, but as Christ has gone before us and set the example, in Him we too find all we need to follow Him and not fall into sin and temptation.
29) We can come boldly to the throne of grace for mercy and grace to help in troubled times. Read Hebrews 10:19-23.

Hebrews Chapter 3

Answers

1) The brethren.
2) Consider. The Strong's Greek Definition reads; to behold, to perceive, discover, to understand.
3) The Apostle and High Priest of our faith, Jesus Christ.
4) God the Father, who appointed Him.
5) Moses.
6) Jesus.
7) God.
8) He was a faithful servant.
9) His own, the church.
10) We hold fast our confidence to the end.
11) If ...you will hear His voice.

   The children of Israel had hardened their hearts to God, yet time and time again God had shown the children of Israel He was more than able to care for them, protect them, provide for their needs. Instead of trusting Him, they rejected Him (Num. 14:11). Just as those in Moses' day were not able to inherit the Promised Land (Num. 14:26-32) that God had spoken to Abraham 430 years earlier (Gen. 12:5-7; 13:14-17), those hearing this letter were also in danger of rejecting the salvation offered to them through Christ Jesus.

12) They hardened their hearts
13) Vs. 7: To hear God. Vs. 8: Do not harden your hearts. Vs. 9: Tested and tried God.

   Vs. 9: God's works for forty years. Vs. 10: In their hearts. Vs. 10: God's ways.

   Vs. 11: "They shall not enter My rest".

14) When we harden our hearts. It is not that they did not know, remember verse 9, it is that they chose to reject. Read Romans 1:28a, 32. They chose to not retain, *keep, remember,* those things that they knew. They made a choice. Read Romans 1:32

again. They knew the righteous judgment; still they chose to practice evil.

15) Unbelief.

16) Departing from the living God.

17) To exhort one another daily (address, comfort, instruct, admonish, strengthen, teach) lest we become hardened through the deceitfulness of sin.

18) Partakers of Christ, if we hold fast to the end.

19) The children of Israel.

20) They died in the wilderness, unable to enter the Promised Land and the rest God had offered them. Verses 18, 19 tell us they did not obey God (verse 17; they sinned) because of unbelief.

21) The Promised Land and eventually, rest from their enemies.

22) Because of unbelief.

23) Unbelief.

Do you struggle with unbelief? Maybe in your relationships or your finances? Maybe just really believing that God *is* able to save *and* willing to forgive? Let Him know you're having a hard time, He knows it anyway. Confess that you understand that you're not really trusting Him. That you *do* want to enter His rest and His peace. It is hard at times to live by faith, trusting in what you can't always touch or see. All of us have had these struggles, but we always have a choice in what we believe. God loves you, He cares for you, and He will always help you.

Hebrews Chapter 4

Answers

1) A promise of entering His rest.
2) The gospel.
3) The children of Israel.
4) Yes.
5) It was not accompanied with faith. We exercise our faith when we remain steadfast in the midst of turmoil, trusting that God Is over all of our circumstances and remaining in Him. It is in the trials and tribulations that our faith is 'worked out'. If we say we have faith and then turn away when the trials come, we reveal that we have no faith and the word which we heard dies away. Read Matthew 13:20,21.
6) Those who have believed.
7) A) Did not enter. B) Because of disobedience C) Today. D) A rest.
8) Diligent, lest we also fall away because of disobedience or unbelief.
9) To work at, painstaking, careful, persevering. For to labor earnestly with haste and speed; to endeavor, a forward movement.
10) I am sure I would do well to do better in all areas, but if I had to pick a few I would say keeping the faith when trials get truly overwhelming, making quiet time with God so I might hear Him instead of doing all the talking, and remembering that I am truly and completely forgiven and free in Christ Jesus.
11) Living and powerful, sharper than any two-edged sword, piercing to the division of soul and spirit, and of joints and marrow; discerning thoughts and intents of the heart.

    The Strong's Greek definition of discernment includes; to separate, to pick out, to choose. To determine, resolve, to pronounce an opinion concerning right and wrong, to judge. Keep in mind it is not our opinion, but it is the Word of God that is discerning. It is in Him and through Him that we get direction, and it is His word that we measure all of our actions and deeds, choices and judgments against.

12) No.
13) Give an account. This is not the white throne judgment reserved for those who have rejected Christ.
14) A: A High Priest. B: Jesus the Son of God. C: He has passed through the heavens (the veil?).
15) Hold fast our confession of faith.
16) Sympathizes with our weaknesses because He was also tempted.
17) A: All who come to Him. B: Makes intercession.
18) Come boldly to the throne of grace that we may obtain mercy and find grace to help in our times of need. Hallelujah!!!

Hebrews Chapter 5

Answers

1) A) Taken B) Among men C) Is appointed D) Men E) Gifts and sacrifices F) Sin.
2) He is also subject to weakness.
3) To offer sacrifices for his own sin.
4) No.
5) God.
6) No.
7) A: God the Father. B: You are a Priest forever.
8) A: God. B: God. C: Because of His godly fear.

   This fear contains an attitude of worship, reverence, service, and devoutness. In keeping with that attitude, as Christ again gives us an example of how we seek and pray to the Father, another example Christ exhorts us with is in 1 Cor. 11:27-31. We need to be examining ourselves and how we hold our Savior and our God. Is our relationship directed by reverence and love and awe? Or are we getting lazy and maybe a little too comfortable and careless in our walk, in our fellowship, and in our communion with our God. Something worth thinking about I think.

9) Obedience, through the things He suffered.
10) Perfected.
11) The author, or source, of eternal salvation to all who obey.
12) God.
13) Dull of hearing.
14) Teachers.
15) A: Someone to teach them. B: The first principles of the oracles of God. C: Milk, not solid food.
16) Unskilled in the word of righteousness, a babe.
17) Mature, those who are growing in knowledge and wisdom. Those who, through faith, are exercising what they believe.
18) Through use.

Hebrews Chapter 6

Answers

1) The discussion of elementary principles, to perfection, maturity.
2) A) Repentance from dead works. B) Faith. C) Doctrine of baptisms. D) The Laying on of hands. E) Resurrection of the dead. F) Eternal judgment.
3) All scripture is given by inspiration of God, and is profitable for doctrine, reproof, correction, instruction in righteousness, that the man of God may be complete, thoroughly equipped for every good work.
4) A) Once enlightened. B) Tasted the heavenly gift. C) Partakers of the Holy Spirit.
   D) Tasted the good word of God. E) Powers.
5) To renew them again to repentance.
6) Crucifying Him again and putting Him to an open shame.
7) I believe it would be someone who claimed to be a follower. It makes our Savior look weak, unable to keep and to save. Destroys our credibility, leaving those outside the faith to question the authenticity and absoluteness of scripture, and contributes to that wrong idea of being able to 'save ourselves'. As you read through scripture and history it is apparent how Satan tried to destroy the church from the outside, i.e. much persecution and death, yet it only served to make the church stronger. Now, as well, it would seem that he would try to destroy the church from the inside, and unfortunately has accomplished much damage. But never forget, it Is God's church, and the gates of hell will not prevail against it. No matter what!!!
8) A) It receives blessings from God. B) It is rejected and near to being burned.
9) Confident of better things concerning them.
10) Their work and labor of love.
11) How they have done, and continue to minister to the saints.

12) That the same diligence they apply in the ministry, they apply to being assured of their salvation in Jesus Christ.
13) Those that endure and keep the faith.
14) 25 years.
15) Strong consolation and hope to lay hold of the hope set before us, comfort.
16) As an anchor for the soul, both sure and steadfast.
17) Jesus Christ.
18) God Almighty.

Hebrews Chapter 7

Answers

1) King of Salem, priest of the Most High God, met Abraham returning from the slaughter and blessed him, received a tithe from Abraham, is translated 'king of righteousness, and 'king of Salem, without father, without mother, without genealogy, having neither beginning of days nor end of life, made like the Son of God, remains a priest continually.
2) Abram heard that his nephew, Lot, had been taken captive.
3) Abram brought back all the goods, his nephew Lot and all of his goods, as well as the women and the people.
4) He gave him a tithe of all.
5) Abraham gave to Melchizedek a tenth part of all.
6) King of righteousness, and king of Salem, which means 'king of peace'.
7) He is without father, mother, without genealogy.
8) Those seeking the priesthood must be listed, their genealogy registered, or they are excluded as defiled.
9) ...but made like the Son of God, remains a priest continually.
10) Pertaining to the Levites, they may enter at 25 years of age and must retire at 50.
11) The order of Melchizedek.
12) The sons of Levi.
13) They receive tithes.
14) Their brethren.
15) Melchizedek
16) The law
17) Another priest not called according to the order of Aaron.
18) A change (removing) of the law. Remember, the Levites taught the law. If the priesthood is removed, so is the law in its form. This law is based on man's ability to meet its requirements, which we cannot do. We needed a better way, a permanent way, and a way was made for us in Jesus. Remember Romans 8:3, 4; 7:6.

19) Jesus.
20) The tribe of Judah.
21) No.
22) The tribe of Levi, the Levites.
23) The law.
24) Because of its weakness and un-profitableness.
25) A fleshly commandment, in that it was based on man's ability to meet all the requirements.
26) The law made nothing perfect.
27) Met the righteous requirements of the law.
28) Believers. Who do not walk according to the flesh, but according to the *Spirit.*
29) There is now no condemnation to those who are in Christ Jesus, who do not walk according to the flesh, but according to the Spirit. Again this is conditional, John 8: 10-12. Not all are children of God.
30) With.
31) You are a priest forever, according to the order of Melchizedek.
32) He has come not according to the law of a fleshly commandment, but according to the power of an endless life. Roman's 8:12-14; Ephesians 1:19, 20.
33) They died, leaving the need for a replacement, and then another, and then another, and so it continued.
34) Because He continues forever, He has no end. Remember the order of Melchezidek; he had no beginning, no end.
35) Offer up sacrifices for His sin.
36) For their sin, and the sins of the people.
37) Offered up a sacrifice for the people once and for all. There is now no more need for another sacrifice. The blood of Christ paid the debt in full, once and for all.
38) As men who have weaknesses.
39) The Son, Jesus Christ, who has been perfected forever.

Hebrews Chapter 8

Answers

1) We have such a High Priest.
2) Jesus Christ.
3) A) With an oath. B) Without an oath.
4) A) By death from continuing. B) Has an unchangeable priesthood. C) Save to the uttermost those who come to God through Him. D) Is holy, harmless, undefiled, and separate from sinners. E) Higher than the heavens. F) To offer up sacrifices for the sins of the people. G) Men who have weakness. H) Perfected forever.
5) For every high priest is appointed to offer both gifts and sacrifices.
6) Himself as an offering and a sacrifice to God, for a sweet smelling aroma.
7) A) The tribe of Levi, or, the Levites. B) The tribe of Judah.
8) The copy and shadow of the heavenly things.
9) The tabernacle according to the pattern God had shown him on the mountain.
10) The first covenant had faults.
11) The children of Israel did not obey God. They did not continue in, or keep, His covenant.
12) Write them on our hearts. You can also read Deut. 10:15, 16.
13) Tablets of stone.
14) "I will give you a new heart and put a new spirit within you; I will take the heart of stone out of your flesh and give you a heart of flesh. I will put My Spirit within you and cause you to walk in My statutes, and you will keep My judgments and do them".

Read verse 11. Now this does not mean that we do not have a responsibility to share the gospel and fulfill the *great commission, Matt. 28:18-20;* Acts 1:8. It does remind us that back in the Old Testament times the people received God's commandments and statutes only when the law was read, and later, through the Pharisees in the synagogue. Now, we all have access to the Father through the Son. Now, we have the Holy Spirit to convict us (if we are His) and guide us as much as we, each of us, are willing, are yielded, and have the desire to seek out and live in the light of God's grace and truths. John 14:15-17, 16:13;

2 Timothy 3:16, 17.

15) Made the first one obsolete.

Hebrews Chapter 9

Answers

1) The lamp stand, the table of showbread. The Sanctuary.
2) Holy of Holies.
3) Ark of the Covenant. It contained the golden pot of manna, Exodus 16:31–34; The tablet of the covenant, that is, the two tablets that had the 10 commandments on them, Exodus 25:16, 21,22; Deuteronomy 10:2; And Aaron's rod that budded Numbers 17:8-11.
4) He went in alone, once a year.
5) To bring the blood offering that he would offer for himself and for the people for their sins committed in ignorance.
6) To make him who performed these perfect, with regard to conscience, inward corruption.
7) Foods, drinks, various washings and fleshly ordinances.
8) Jesus Christ.
9) A) Jesus Christ. B) His own blood, body. C) Eternal redemption. D) There is now no longer a need for continued sacrifices, or works (as in the law), or rituals. 1 John 1:7,9. *It is finished.........* *John 19:30.*
10) Works, practices and rituals of the law.
11) A) The new covenant. B) His death. C) The transgressions committed under the first covenant. D) The promise of the eternal inheritance. *Salvation.*
12) When the one who wrote it dies.
13) Blood.
14) A) He spoke every part of the law to the people. B) He took the blood of calves and goats, mixed them and sprinkled both the book and the people. Both the people and the book were dedicated into God's service. C) The people answered in one voice and said, "All the words which the Lord has said we will do."
15) Jesus said, "This is the blood of the new covenant, My blood, which is shed for many for the remission of sins."

16) The tabernacle and all the vessels of the ministry.
17) Without shedding of blood there is no remission, of sin.
18) The cross. Jesus gave His life for us.
19) Make intercession for us.
20) He died, was raised, is at the right hand of God, and makes intercession for us.
21) Offer Himself often, as the high priest made offerings every year. He would have had to suffer often since the foundation of the world.
22) A) Once at the end of the ages. B) To put away sin. C) Himself.
23) To die once, and then the judgment.
24) Once. As men die once, so Christ died once.
25) Salvation

Hebrews Chapter 10

Answers

1) Make those who offer these sacrifices perfect.
2) Reminded them of their sins.
3) Take away sins.
4) To do God's will.
5) That we would believe on the One whom He has sent and have eternal life.
6) God took away the first covenant to establish the second.
7) Because the first covenant had faults in that it was based on man's ability.
8) God's will.
9) We have been sanctified (when we believe and receive) through the offering of the body of Jesus Christ.
10) A) He is standing. B) He offers the same sacrifices. C) Take away sins.
11) A) Jesus Christ. B) One sacrifice for sins forever. C) Sat down at the right hand of God. D) All that needed to be done was now done. *It is finished.*
12) Those that are being sanctified; set apart.
13) Because we have been forgiven, completely. See again verse 17.
14) The veil that separated the Holy place from the Most Holy Place.
15) It was the room where the Ark of the Covenant sat with the mercy seat and God's presence was there.
16) A) Having our hearts sprinkled from an evil conscience. B) Our bodies washed with pure water. C) By the blood of Jesus, and by the washing of water by the word, Eph. 5:26.
17) A) With a sincere heart. B) The confession of our hope. C) Consider one another. D) In the sure assurance of faith. E) Without wavering. F) To stir up love and good works.
18) First I think we need to be mindful of the affect we can and do have on one another, to good and to bad. We can build

up and encourage, or tear down and discourage. Second, as we are aware of one another, (we shared in our Galatians and Ephesians Study that we should be more than casual acquaintances, committed to and involved with one another) we should be encouraging and praying, teaching and training, united and effective in the body of Christ. Committing one another to service and ministry as God calls us. Bearing with one another, enduring with one another, that together we might truly be a people set apart for God and effective in the good works He has called us to.

19) Assemble together.
20) Exhorting one another. Encouraging, correcting, teaching, restoring, and serving.
21) As we see the Day approaching.
22) Christ's return.
23) When once we have received the knowledge of the truth and continue to sin willfully. To sin willfully means to do so not out of ignorance, but intentionally. If someone has received the good news and chooses to reject it, there is nothing else. They have condemned themselves. For some understanding of what our choices can cost us, read Matt. 13: 53-58, especially verse 58. When we reject what God in Christ has afforded us, we lose.
24) A certain fearful expectation of judgment.
25) Enemies of God.
26) They are put to death without mercy on the testimony of two witnesses.
27) A) Trample the Son of God underfoot. B) Counted the blood of the covenant (Christ's blood) a common thing. C) Insulted the Spirit of grace.
28) A) "Vengeance is Mine, I will repay. The Lord will judge His people." B) " Do not fear what man can do to you. Fear Him who has the power to cast you into hell."
29) Recall the former days.
30) How they endured a great struggle with suffering.
31) They were at times made a spectacle by both reproaches and tribulations.

32) They had compassion on Paul and others suffering for the faith, and allowed themselves to be ridiculed and having their goods plundered. They were *in the fight, being directly affected,* not consoling from afar and untouched; a big difference. 1 Pet. 4:13, 14; Matt. 5:12.
33) They have a better and enduring position in heaven.
34) Cast away their confidence.
35) In Christ Jesus and His salvation. God *is* at work.

Hebrews Chapter 11

Answers

1) It is the substance of things hoped for, the evidence of things not seen.
2) Faith.
3) Those believers of the Old Testament.
4) A good testimony from God. They pleased God, were declared righteous.
5) Of the things which are visible.
6) God spoke everything into existence.
7) He offered it in faith, in obedience, believing God.
8) Death. That he pleased God.
9) Without faith it is impossible to please God.
10) They must believe that *He is,* and a rewarder of those who diligently seek Him.
11) A thing not yet seen.
12) Rain.
13) Godly fear.
14) An heir of the righteousness according to faith.
15) He left his homeland and his family and went out to a place he did not know.
16) As in a foreign country.
17) They understood that their stay was temporary in that they did not set up a permanent residence.
18) The city which has foundations, whose builder and maker is God.
19) The New Jerusalem.
20) Strength to conceive.
21) Because she judged Him faithful who had promised. She believed.
22) Abraham.
23) He was past the age to be able to get Sarah pregnant.

24) A) In the faith. B) Received the promises. C) They were assured of them and embraced them. D) Strangers and pilgrims on the earth.
25) That they seek a homeland.
26) Heaven.
27) He offered up his only son Isaac.
28) To see if they are truly His.
29) That God was able to raise him, his son Isaac, up from the dead.
30) God will surely visit you and bring you out of this land to the land He swore to Abraham.
31) Moses.
32) To kill all the male babies born to the Hebrews.
33) By faith.
34) A passing pleasure.
35) Faith.
36) Those who did not believe.
37) They obtained a good testimony through faith.
38) The promise, not for faith and righteousness, but that they should not be made perfect, *read complete,* apart from, or in a different way, than us. That is, the coming of Jesus Christ and His kingdom. The Cross.

Hebrews Chapter 12

Answers

1) The saints mentioned above.
2) Sin is a willful act, a choice to disobey God. A weight is something that hinders, not necessarily bad or wrong in and of itself, but gets in the way. It is a distraction. I would submit that because in and of itself it is (seemingly) harmless, we tend to give no thought to what it can and does cost us. Again, all things are lawful, but not all are edifying,
3) Let us run with endurance the race set before us.
4) Looking unto the author and finisher of our faith.
5) Jesus Christ.
6) A) Jesus Christ. B) How He endured such hostility from sinners against Him. C) Lest we become weary and discouraged.
7) Illegitimate and not sons.
8) That we may be partakers of His holiness.
9) The peaceable fruit of righteousness.
10) Peace with all peoples, and holiness, without which no one will see the Lord. Now this might seem like a simple thing and easily overlooked or dismissed. But really think. When the world sees us angry, judgmental, bickering over things that have no eternal value, do they see God in us? When we are holding grudges, gossiping about others, and belittling another's point of view? How likely is it that such a person will have much credibility when he or she sets out to share the gospel. Jesus has given us every example on forgiveness, turning the other cheek, going the extra miles, not going after His accusers but left it all with the Father. Being peaceable with all peoples is difficult. But in discipline, in obedience, in His love and grace, we can. We must.
11) A) Fall short of the grace of God (rejecting grace for works). B) Bitterness springs up causing trouble and by this defiling many (to contaminate, soil, pollute). C) Any fornicator or profane person (sexually immoral).

12) Come down upon Mount Sinai in the sight of the people.
13) They would be put to death. A) Boldly. B) No.
14) They were afraid.
15) Do not fear.
16) God has come to test you that His fear may be before you so that you may not sin.
17) They did not enter into the Promised Land because they rejected God.
18) A certain expectation of judgment.
19) "Not only the earth, but also heaven."
20) The things which cannot be shaken. Remember Matthew 24:35. "Heaven and earth will pass away, but My words will by no means pass away".
21) A new heaven and a new earth. Revelation 21:1, "Now I saw a new heaven and a new earth, for the first heaven and the first earth had passed away".
22) We have *grace,* not only to abide in, but to apply in our service to God and in our ministry to one another. To love and serve in reverence and praise, remembering that we have our very being from Him alone.

    It is an amazing and wonderful thing to come boldly to the throne room of God, yet I worry sometimes that we can get too comfortable, even lazy in our relationship towards God. As much as our Father is loving and forgiving and patient, let us never forget the *majesty and power* of the One who is on the throne. Maybe it's just me.
23) But as He who called you is holy, you also be holy in all your conduct, because it is written,
    "Be holy, for I am holy."

Hebrews Chapter 13

Answers

1) A) Let brotherly love continue. B) Do not forget to entertain strangers. C) Remember the prisoners as if chained with them, not as just a passing thought.
2) What we have.
3) "I will never leave you nor forsake you."
4) The Lord is my Helper, I will not fear, and what can man do to me.
5) While as I was a sinner, Christ died for me and saved me.
6) Pastor's, teachers, elders, etc.
7) He is the same yesterday, today and forever.
8) If we are not living in the blessed assurance of God's grace, something we could not earn, we will never truly experience His peace, His rest. There will always be someone insisting that we must do *this* or we have to do *that. How could we ever be effective in our service or in our ministry, or even in our homes when we feel continually disqualified?* Yet *on the solid rock I stand.* Jesus Christ. Not by my works, but by His grace alone.
9) Continually.
10) When we *do good* and *share.* Notice the word <u>sacrifice.</u> It is not always going to be easy. If it is always easy, then it is not a sacrifice.
11) Pray for us.
12) That we would be made *complete* in every good work to *do His will.*
13) Bear (endure, accept something as a duty or responsibility) his exhortation, do not fall away but be strong, steadfast, and brave.
14) Grace be with you all, Amen.

Thank you for a wonderful study!
May we always be pleasing in His sight.

Bibliography

The New King James Bible

The Holy Bible, King James Version
World Bible Publishers; Iowa Falls, Iowa
Copyright DeVore and Sons, Inc., 1979

Strong, James. *The New Strong's Exhaustive Concordance of the Bible*. Nashville: Thomas Nelson. 1990

Webster. *The New World College Dictionary*.
Third Edition. New York: Macmillan. 1989.